Contents

Meet the
Lion

Lions are fierce and strong cats. Most work together in groups called **prides**. A pride can have as many as 40 lions, but most have about 15 lions. A pride usually includes one to three males, several females called lionesses, and their cubs. The females all belong to the same family. Males and females have different roles. The males defend their **territory** and pride, while the females are responsible for hunting and raising cubs.

The male lion is the only member of the cat family to grow a **mane**. It covers the head, neck, and chest. The color of the mane gets darker with age. Manes help the males look fierce and may protect their throats in a fight.

A lion's roar can be heard from 5 miles (8 kilometers) away. Lions roar to warn other males to stay away from their territory. The roar is also a signal to the pride.

All About Lions

Lions are members of the cat, or *felidae*, family of **mammals**. Throughout the world, there are 41 **species** of cats. Lions have two subspecies, the African and the Asiatic.

African lions live mainly in the eastern and southern parts of Africa. White lions, with all-white manes, live in parts of South Africa. Male lions that do not grow manes at all live in one region of Kenya. Along the Upper Nile River, some lions live in caves. There, the males hunt, and the females remain with the cubs.

Asiatic lions now live only in India, in Gir National Park. They are smaller than African lions. Asiatic lions have thicker coats and scruffier manes. Asiatic males travel alone. They do not live in prides as African males do.

The Swahili word for lion is simba.

Comparing Big Cats

The lion is one of the largest cat species in the world. Only tigers are larger. Lions can run fast for short amounts of time, but they are slower than tigers, jaguars, and cheetahs. The lion uses its strength to hunt and catch its prey because it does not have the speed of other animals. Lionesses are lighter and faster than the males and do most of the hunting.

Jaguar

+ **Length:**
  7–9 feet
  (213–274 centimeters)
  including tail
+ **Weight:**
  100–250 pounds
  (45–113 kilograms)
+ **Speed:**
  Up to 40 miles per hour
  (64 kilometers
  per hour)

Lion

+ **Length:**
  6.5–9 feet
  (198–274 cm)
  including tail
+ **Weight:**
  265–420 lbs
  (120–190 kg)
+ **Speed:**
  Up to 35 mph (56 kph)

Tiger

+ **Length:**
  7.5–10.8 feet
  (260–330 cm)
  including tail
+ **Weight:**
  220–675 pounds
  (100–306 kg)
+ **Speed:**
  Up to 40 miles per hour
  (64 kph)

Leopard

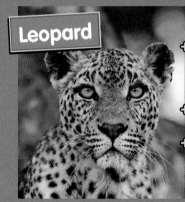

+ **Length:**
  6.5–9 feet
  (198–274 cm)
  including tail
+ **Weight:**
  66–176 lbs (30–80 kg)
+ **Speed:**
  Up to 57 mph (92 kph)

Cheetah

+ **Length:**
  6–7 feet
  (183–213 cm)
  including tail
+ **Weight:**
  77–143 lbs (35–65 kg)
+ **Speed:**
  Up to 70 mph
  (112 kph)

Cougar

+ **Length:**
  5–9 feet
  (152–274 cm)
  including tail
+ **Weight:**
  Up to 150 lbs (68 kg)
+ **Speed:**
  Up to 35 mph (56 kph)

Lion History

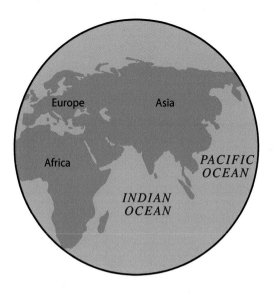

The first **ancestor** of the lion lived in Africa about 1.5 million years ago. **Fossils** of the animal show that it was similar to the lions and tigers of today.

Lions once lived all over Africa, Asia, North America, northern South America, and Europe. Scientists have found lion fossils across France, China, and Peru. Lions became **extinct** almost 2,000 years ago in Europe. They continued to live in Asia until about 150 years ago.

People have hunted lions over the years, and human activity has destroyed much of the lions' **habitat**. There are fewer lions in the world than ever before. In Africa, there were about 200,000 lions living in nature about 100 years ago. Now, there are less than 30,000 left.

DWINDLING DOWN

Lions are extinct in 26 countries, and only 7 countries have more than 1,000 lions living in nature.

The Barbary lion from northern Africa is already extinct in nature.

Where Lions Live

Although lions have the name "king of the jungle," they do not live there. Lions live on plains or **savanna,** areas with tall grass, thick bush, and a few woodland areas. Lions are **predators**, so they need to live in places with many **prey** animals that they can hunt for food.

Lions will live and hunt in the same area for many years. Their territory covers an area of about 100 to 200 square miles (259 to 518 square kilometers). Male lions mark their territory with their scent. This lets other animals know to keep out.

The lion's tawny coat is good protection in the tall grass of the savanna.

TAKING IT EASY

Lions spend most of their days resting, with short bursts of activity during hunting.

Lion
Features

Lions have special **adaptations** to help them hunt. They move fast to chase down prey. Their claws are designed to grip prey so it cannot escape. Lions have excellent eyesight to help them hunt in the dark.

Getting Closer

① Legs
- Uses strong muscles in front legs to push prey to the ground
- Can reach speeds of 50 miles (81 kilometers) per hour
- Can leap almost 36 feet (10.9 meters)

② Eyes
- Good night vision
- Can see eight times better than the average human
- Round pupils
- Second eyelid cleans and protects eye

③ Teeth
- 30 very sharp teeth
- Swallows food in chunks instead of chewing
- **Canine** teeth cut and tear
- Hinged jaw opens as wide as 11 inches (28 centimeters)

④ Paws
- Soft pads to sneak up on prey
- Heels do not touch the ground while walking
- Sharp, curved claws help hold onto prey
- Claws up to 1.5 inches (3.8 centimeters) long
- Claws can be **retracted** when not in use

What Do Lions Eat?

Lions are **carnivores**. On the African savanna, there are many animals for lions to hunt. Common food choices include impala, warthog, and water buck. Lions also eat small rodents and hares.

Hunting is done mostly at night or in the early morning. The lions work as a group to **stalk** and kill prey. Lions are good at hiding, and they are very patient.

Lions eat their prey at once and then may not hunt again for several days. A lion will eat an average of 15 pounds (7 kilograms) of meat in one sitting.

Lions are **scavengers**. They will often steal kill from other animals or eat any dead animal that they find. Lions eat in a crouching or lying-down position. They tend to drag their food away from open areas.

Lions prey on large mammals such as zebras, wildebeests, and even giraffes and buffalo.

BEWARE THE LION

Lions can be inactive for about 20 hours a day. This can make prey mistakenly believe they are in no danger.

Lion
Life Cycle

Both females and males are ready to mate at 2 years of age. They mate at any time of the year. Lion cubs are born after about 110 days. The average litter size is between one and six cubs. A lioness can have a litter about every other year.

Birth to 2 Weeks

When lion cubs are born, they weigh between 2 and 4 pounds (1 and 2 kilograms) and measure 1 foot (30.5 centimeters) in length. They have gray, woolly coats with spots. This keeps them **camouflaged** from predators. Cubs are born with their eyes closed and cannot see. Only one in eight cubs survives to adulthood. Cubs born in a pride have a better chance at surviving than those born to a lioness on her own.

Females in a pride often give birth around the same time. They hide their cubs away from the pride, and then introduce them when they are about 6 weeks old. A lioness cares for her cubs until they are about 2 years old.

2 Years and Older

The females hunt and are now able to mate. The males defend their pride and territory. Lions may drive some males out of the pride, leaving them to fight for their own pride. Older lionesses may force some females out of the pride. These lions become **nomad lions** that must travel to find a new pride. Lions can live about 15 years in nature.

2 Weeks to 2 Years

After three weeks, the cubs open their eyes. Milk teeth soon appear. Cubs drink milk from any female in the pride, not just their mother. Their eyes turn color from blue to amber or brown by 3 months of age. Cubs spend their time playing and learning. They help with hunting at 1 year of age. Males begin to grow manes at about 18 months of age.

Conservation of Lions

Today, most lions live in protected areas such as national parks or **sanctuaries**. Even though they are the top predator in the area, they still face dangers that put their lives at risk. One reason for putting lions in protected areas is loss of habitat. Another reason is starvation. If there are not enough prey animals in an area, lions will starve to death. In some parts of Africa, hunters have killed so many prey animals that lions have to kill farm animals as food. As a result, farmers often hunt and poison the lions.

The lion population is also at risk due to **poaching**. Hunters kill male lions for sport or to sell their skin and manes for rugs. In some very poor regions of Africa, people still hunt lions for food.

ALMOST GONE

The **IUCN** believes that the African and Asian lion populations are both at risk. Members of the IUCN work to keep lions from becoming extinct.

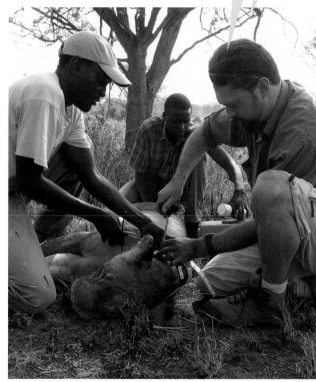

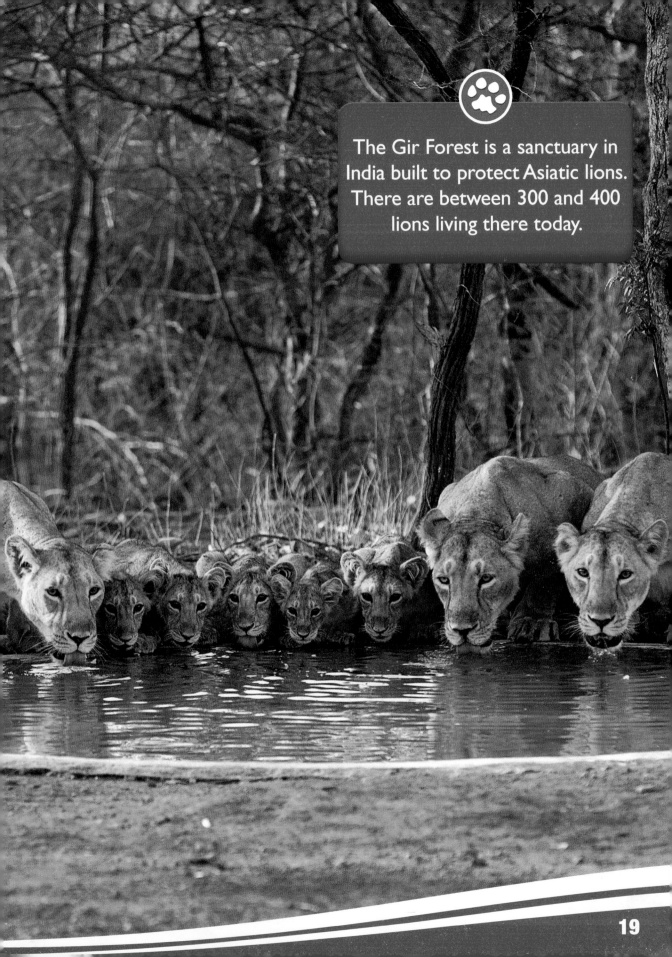

The Gir Forest is a sanctuary in India built to protect Asiatic lions. There are between 300 and 400 lions living there today.

Myths and Legends

For thousands of years, lions have been symbols of courage, strength, and power. Many countries, such as Albania, England, Ethiopia, and Singapore, use the lion as their national symbol. Lions have also become popular characters in movies and novels. There are statues of lions in many cities.

All over the world, people tell stories about lions. One African legend tells how, long ago, the lion had wings like those of a giant bat. It could swoop down on its prey from high up in the sky. The lion's ability to fly came from the bones of his prey, which he stored in a nearby cave. One day, a cunning bullfrog discovered the cave and destroyed the magic bones. The lion's wings disappeared. From that day on, the lion had to hunt his prey on foot.

When a lion roars, Africans believe it is saying, "he inchi ya nani—yangu, yangu, yangu." This means, "Whose land is this? It is mine, mine, mine!"

What Does a Lion Do?

The males, females, and cubs in a pride of lions all work together. Each performs a specific role within the group. You can compare the duties of the members in a pride to understand how they work together in different roles.

Materials Needed: You will need a large piece of paper and colored markers.

STEP 1 Draw three circles, using a different color for each. Make sure that all the circles overlap at the sides and in the center. Label each one with a different heading: lion, lioness, and cub.

STEP 2 Review the information in this book, and search the internet to find out about the roles of each lion family member.

STEP 3 In each circle, list the duties of each member of the pride.
Where the duties are the same, such as the males and females both helping with the hunt, write that in the parts of the circle that overlap. If males, females, and cubs all share a duty, write that in the center where all the circles overlap. When you are finished, you will see how each lion helps the pride survive.

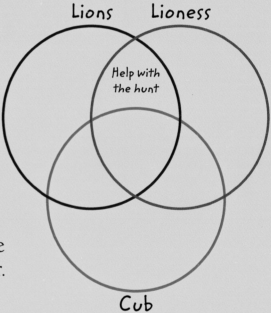

Lions   Lioness

Help with
the hunt

Cub

5 Know Your FACTS

Test your knowledge of lions.

1 On which two continents are lions found today?

2 What is the name given to a group of lions?

3 How does a lion spend most of its day?

4 About how old are male cubs when they can be driven from the pride?

5 What are three threats to lions that live in nature?

ANSWERS

1 Africa and Asia

2 A pride

3 Resting

4 About 2 years old

5 Loss of habitat, poaching, and starvation

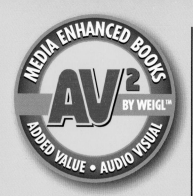

AV² provides enriched content that supplements and complements this book. Weigl's AV² books strive to create inspired learning and engage young minds in a total learning experience.

Your AV² Media Enhanced books come alive with...

Audio
Listen to sections of the book read aloud.

Video
Watch informative video clips.

Embedded Weblinks
Gain additional information for research.

Try This!
Complete activities and hands-on experiments.

Key Words
Study vocabulary, and complete a matching word activity.

Quizzes
Test your knowledge.

Slide Show
View images and captions, and prepare a presentation.

... and much, much more!

Go to **www.av2books.com**, and enter this book's unique code.

BOOK CODE

G36672

AV² by Weigl brings you media enhanced books that support active learning.

Published by AV² by Weigl
350 5ᵗʰ Avenue, 59ᵗʰ Floor
New York, NY 10118
Websites: www.av2books.com   www.weigl.com

Library of Congress Cataloging-in-Publication Data

Daly, Ruth, 1962- author.
 Lion / Ruth Daly.
    pages cm. -- (Big cats)
 Includes index.
 ISBN 978-1-4896-0926-7 (hardcover : alk. paper) -- ISBN 978-1-4896-0927-4 (softcover : alk. paper) -- ISBN 978-1-4896-0928-1 (ebk.) -- ISBN 978-1-4896-0929-8 (ebk.)
 1. Lion--Juvenile literature. I. Title.
 QL737.C23D345 2015
 599.757--dc23

2014004316

Printed in the United States of America in North Mankato, Minnesota
1 2 3 4 5 6 7 8 9 0 18 17 16 15 14

032014
WEP150314

Editor Heather Kissock   Design Terry Paulhus

Photo Credits
Weigl acknowledges Getty Images, Alamy, and Corbis as its primary photo suppliers for this title.

Big Cats

Lion

Written by
Ruth Daly

MEDIA ENHANCED BOOKS
AV2 BY WEIGL
ADDED VALUE • AUDIO VISUAL

www.av2books.com